WHAT IS RELIGION?

Bobbie Kalman

🌴 Crabtree Publishing Company

www.crabtreebooks.com

Created by Bobbie Kalman

Fear separates. Love brings us together.
Do not fear the differences in others.
Let kindness and love overcome your fears.

Author and Editor-in-Chief
Bobbie Kalman

Text and Photo Research
Tammy Ovens

Editor
Kathy Middleton

Proofreader
Crystal Sikkens

Design
Bobbie Kalman
Katherine Berti
Samantha Crabtree (cover)

Production coordinator
Katherine Berti

Photographs and reproductions
© BigStockPhoto.com: pages 19 (middle right), 22 (bottom left), 23 (middle)
© Dreamstime.com: page 23 (bottom right)
© Alfredo Rodriguez: *Courage His Only Weapon*: page 29 (top left); *When Grandfather Speaks*: page 28
© Shutterstock.com: covers, pages 1, 3, 4, 5, 6, 7, 8, 9, 10, 11, 12 (top and bottom), 13, 14 (except bottom left), 15 (except top left), 16, 17, 18, 19 (except middle right), 20, 21, 22 (except bottom left), 23 (top and bottom left), 24, 25, 26, 27, 28 (top), 29 (except top left), 30
Other images by Circa Art

Library and Archives Canada Cataloguing in Publication

Kalman, Bobbie, 1947-
    What is religion? / Bobbie Kalman.

(Our multicultural world)
Includes index.
ISBN 978-0-7787-4636-2 (bound).--ISBN 978-0-7787-4651-5 (pbk.)

    1. Religions--Juvenile literature. 2. Religion--Juvenile literature.
I. Title. II. Series: Our multicultural world

BL92.K34 2009   j200   C2009-900653-7

Library of Congress Cataloging-in-Publication Data

Kalman, Bobbie.
  What is religion? / Bobbie Kalman.
      p. cm. -- (Our multicultural world)
  Includes index.
  ISBN 978-0-7787-4651-5 (pbk. : alk. paper) -- ISBN 978-0-7787-4636-2
(reinforced library binding : alk. paper)
  1. Religions--Juvenile literature. 2. Religion--Juvenile literature. I. Title. II.
Series.

  BL92.K36 2009
  200--dc22
                                                                2009003338

Crabtree Publishing Company
www.crabtreebooks.com   1-800-387-7650

Published in Canada
Crabtree Publishing
616 Welland Ave.
St. Catharines, Ontario
L2M 5V6

Published in the United States
Crabtree Publishing
PMB16A
350 Fifth Ave., Suite 3308
New York, NY 10118

Published in the United Kingdom
Crabtree Publishing
White Cross Mills
High Town, Lancaster
LA1 4XS

Published in Australia
Crabtree Publishing
386 Mt. Alexander Rd.
Ascot Vale (Melbourne)
VIC 3032

Contents

What is religion? 4

Religions of the world 6

Holy books 8

Sacred places on Earth 10

The story of Judaism 12

The story of Jesus 14

Many kinds of Christians 16

The story of Islam 18

What is Hinduism? 20

What is Sikhism? 22

What is Buddhism? 24

Religions of East Asia 26

Native American beliefs 28

Respecting one another 30

Glossary and Index 31

Further reading 32

What is religion?

There are things we can see and observe, and then there are things that happen that we cannot figure out. Long ago, people wondered about who made everything they could see on Earth and in the sky. They wanted answers to questions about why things happened the way they did. **Religions** try to answer those questions. A religion is a way of life with a set of beliefs. It is a community of people who share the same beliefs. Not everyone has a religion. About one-sixth of the people on Earth do not belong to a religion. Some of these people believe in God, but they feel they can live good lives without belonging to a religion.

Long ago, people believed that there were invisible gods or spirits in everything. They prayed to these spirits for good weather, food, and safety. Some religions still honor the spirits of nature.

Really big questions!

Religions try to answer some big questions about life.

- How was the world created?
- Why are we here?
- Is there a God? Where is God?
- How can we live the right way?
- What rules should we follow?
- Why do bad things happen?
- What happens when we die?
- How can we be happy?

Different beliefs

Many religions today believe that a supreme being created all living things. They call this being God, Father, Spirit, and many other names. The idea of God is different to everyone. Some religions believe in many gods, and some religions do not believe in any gods. Instead, they teach people to act in ways that will not hurt themselves or others. Religions ask people not to kill, steal, or cheat. They encourage people to forgive, be grateful, and to love one another.

When people want to talk to God, they pray. Some prayers have special words. Other prayers are said in a person's own words.

incense stick

*This girl is offering incense sticks and flowers as part of her prayers. Incense smells good and is believed to **purify**, or clean. Many religions use incense to send prayers or good thoughts.*

5

Religions of the world

There are thousands of religious groups. Each religion has teachers, **holy** books, special celebrations, and places of worship. Food and clothing are often important parts of religions, too. Each religion also has **sacred symbols**. The symbols below **represent**, or stand for, some of the major religions of the world. These symbols are found outside or inside places of worship and in people's homes.

Christianity

The cross is the symbol of Christianity. Christians believe that Jesus Christ is the son of God. Jesus died on a cross.

Islam

The crescent and star are often used to represent Islam. The moon is a symbol of new beginnings. The star reminds Muslims that they are guided by the teachings of Islam.

Judaism

menorah

Star of David

The Star of David and the menorah are both symbols of Judaism. The star of David appears on the flag of Israel. The menorah is a symbol of the Jewish faith.

Hinduism

Hindus chant the sound "Om" or "Aum" when they **meditate**, or sit in silence. Hindus believe that "Om" is the sound from which Earth was created. The symbol on the left is the written word for this sound.

Sikhism

The circle in this Sikh symbol stands for God, who has no beginning or end, like a circle. The two-edged sword at the center stands for truth and freedom. The two swords at the sides stand for balance in life.

Buddhism

This wheel represents the Eightfold Path. Buddhists follow these eight steps to find happiness and peace.

Shinto

torii

Shinto is an old Japanese religion that means "way of the gods." A torii gate is built at the entrance of Shinto **shrines** for the gods to enter.

Confucianism

Confucianism and Taoism are Chinese beliefs. Confucianism teaches people how to treat others, and Taoism is about health and well-being. The **yin-yang** symbol below stands for the opposites in life. They balance each other.

Taoism

yang

yin

dove of peace

The wheel above shows the world religions coming together at the center, where there is a dove. The dove is a symbol of peace. We may have different beliefs, but we can live together peacefully.

Native American beliefs

N

W

E

S

(left) The Medicine Wheel is the symbol of Native American beliefs. It stands for the journey of four directions that each person takes to find his or her own path.

7

Holy books

Each religion has sacred writings or holy books. These sacred writings are about God or are believed to have come from God. They guide people to live better lives. The books and writings tell people how to do what is right and how to treat others with kindness. The names of some holy books or writings are shown in the box on the right.

Names of writings

Christianity: Bible

Judaism: Hebrew Bible (*Tanakh*), Talmud, Haggadah

Islam: Qur'an (Koran)

Buddhism: *Tripitaka*

Hinduism: Vedas, Bhagavad Gita, Upanishads, Puranas

Sikhism: *Guru Granth Sahib*

Taoism: *Tao Te Ching*

This Muslim mother and her daughters are reading the Qur'an together (see page 18).

This Christian girl is reading the Bible to learn more about the life of Jesus (see pages 14-15).

These sacred writings come from Buddha's teachings (see pages 24-25).

Christian Bible

Torah

(above) The Hebrew Bible is part of the Christian Bible. It is called the Old Testament.
(right) The Torah is the most holy part of the Hebrew Bible. It is written on a scroll.

The Haggadah is a book that is read on the first two nights of the Jewish holiday of Passover.

9

Sacred places on Earth

There are places on Earth that people of certain religions visit. Jerusalem is one of the oldest cities in the world, and it is a very sacred place for Jews, Muslims, and Christians. Jerusalem is Israel's largest city and its capital. Jews from all over the world come to pray at the Western Wall, the holiest place in Jerusalem. The Dome of the Rock, the oldest Islamic building that is still standing, is also in Jerusalem. It is shown in the picture, above right. For Christians, the most sacred place in Jerusalem is the Church of the Holy Sepulchre. The church was built on the spot where Christians believe Jesus died.

*(above) Thousands of Jews have come to pray at the Western Wall. The wall is all that remains of a very old **temple**, or place of worship.*

(right) This child is praying where Jesus is believed to have been buried.

The head of the Roman Catholic Church is the Pope. He lives in Vatican City in Rome, Italy. The Roman Catholic religion was the first Christian religion and is the biggest Christian religion in the world today.

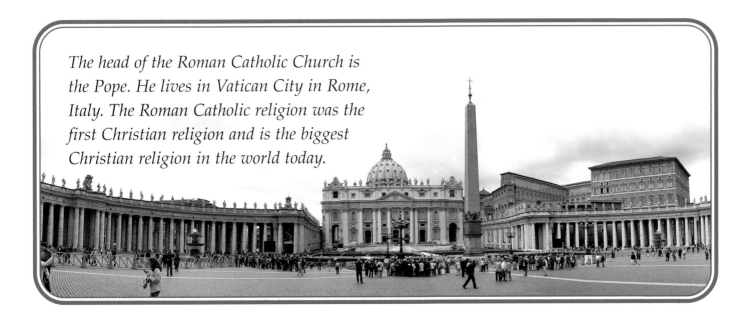

The Ganges River is the most sacred spot for Hindus. Hindus believe that this river flowed down from heaven to Earth. Bathing in the river at dawn is believed to wash away bad actions in a person's life. The two most holy cities on the Ganges River are Banaras and Haridwar.

*Mecca, or Makkah, is in Saudi Arabia. It is the holiest place for Muslims. Muslims believe that they must make at least one **pilgrimage**, or journey, to Mecca. The most sacred spot in Mecca is the Ka'ba, the stone building at the center of the **mosque**, or Muslim place of worship. It is covered in black cloth. When the **pilgrims** arrive at the mosque, they circle seven times around the Ka'ba.*

Ka'ba

The story of Judaism

Judaism is a religion that started almost 4,000 years ago, when people believed in many gods. A man named Abraham believed in one God. He made a **covenant**, or promise, to God to worship only Him. Judaism started with Abraham and was the first religion to worship one God. Moses was another important person in Judaism. He led the Jews out of slavery in Egypt and gave them a set of rules to live by.

The Red Sea parted as Moses led the Jews out of Egypt. The water closed over the Egyptian soldiers when they tried to stop them. The escape from Egypt is called "the Exodus."

From God, Moses received ten rules for his people to follow. These rules were called the Ten Commandments.

The Ten Commandments

The Ten Commandments remind people to worship only one God, to keep His day holy, and to honor their parents. The commandments also forbid cheating, lying, stealing, and wanting what belongs to another. Not killing other people is one of the most important commandments.

The Jewish house of worship is called a temple or **synagogue**.

A Jewish man or boy wears a cap called a **kippa** or **yarmulke** when he prays or enters a synagogue. Some men and boys always wear kippas.

kippas

A **mezuzah** contains a prayer. It is nailed to the doors of homes to honor God and show that He is a part of that home. Some people kiss or touch the mezuzah before they enter a house.

mezuzah

When Jewish boys turn thirteen, they read a part of the Torah in Hebrew at a ceremony called a **Bar Mitzvah**. The ceremony for girls is called a **Bat Mitzvah**.

Important Jewish holidays are Rosh Hashanah, Yom Kippur, and Passover. The main event of Passover is the **Seder**, or special Passover meal.

During Hanukkah, people light a candle on the menorah each night for eight nights. Children receive small gifts and play with toys called dreidels.

dreidels

The story of Jesus

Christianity began with a group of Jews who believed that Jesus was the son of God. Jesus is called the Christ, which means "chosen by God." Christians believe that God sent Jesus to Earth to help people. The story of Jesus is told in the New Testament, the second part of the Christian Bible. Jesus was born in Bethlehem more than 2,000 years ago. Bethlehem is in present-day Israel. Jesus was born into a Jewish family to parents called Mary and Joseph. He was born in a **stable**.

stable

three kings

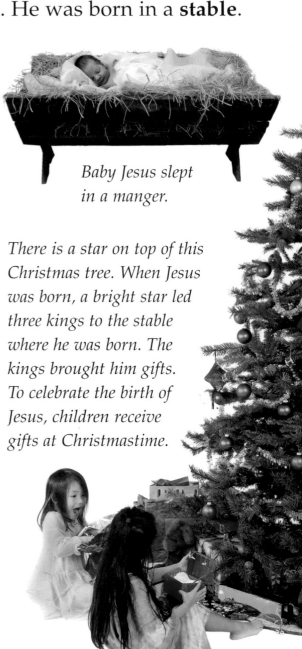

Baby Jesus slept in a manger.

There is a star on top of this Christmas tree. When Jesus was born, a bright star led three kings to the stable where he was born. The kings brought him gifts. To celebrate the birth of Jesus, children receive gifts at Christmastime.

The Christian cross

The New Testament tells stories about Jesus healing the sick and performing miracles. Many people started to call Jesus the **Messiah**, or savior, that they believed God had promised to send them. Some people did not believe that Jesus was the Messiah and thought his ideas were dangerous. Jesus was arrested and was nailed to a cross, where he died. The cross became the symbol of Christianity.

The Resurrection

Three days after Jesus died, the burial cave where his body was laid was found empty. Many people said they saw him alive again. Christians believe that Jesus was **resurrected** by God, or rose from the dead. The Christian holiday of Easter celebrates the resurrection of Jesus. It is the most important holiday of the Christian year.

Easter comes in March or April. Children receive painted or chocolate Easter eggs. Eggs symbolize new life. Sometimes the eggs are hidden in gardens.

 # Many kinds of Christians

Close to one-third of the people on Earth are Christians. Christians follow the teachings of Jesus Christ, but not all Christians follow it in the same way. Christianity has several groups. The three main groups are Roman Catholic, Eastern Orthodox, and Protestant. These groups are divided again into many thousands of different church groups, called **denominations**. All these church groups are Christian, but they have different leaders, different beliefs, and different ways of practicing Christianity.

*Roman Catholic churches are often decorated with beautiful statues and works of art. Many Catholics attend a religious service called a **mass** at least once a week. Mass is also part of ceremonies, such as weddings.*

Eastern Orthodox churches have onion-shaped domes with crosses at their tops to show that they are Christian. The leaders of Eastern Orthodox churches are priests and bishops. Bishops are in charge of a group of churches.

Quick Christian facts

Holy Books: Bible (Old Testament and New Testament)

Places of worship: churches, cathedrals, chapels

Religious leaders: popes, bishops, priests, ministers, pastors

Important holidays: Easter, Christmas

Based on the teachings of: Jesus Christ

Some Christians read the Bible every day to learn about their faith. There are picture Bibles for young children.

*Many people are **baptized**, or become Christians, when they are babies. Water is poured on their heads as part of the ceremony.*

host

*Roman Catholic children receive their First Communion at around the age of seven. Many girls wear white dresses for this event. Roman Catholics believe that the body of Jesus is in the Communion **host** or bread that they eat.*

The story of Islam

Muslims are the followers of Islam. They believe in one God, whose Arabic name is *Allah*. Muslims believe that they are on Earth to give their lives to Allah and to live in a peaceful way. Islam is based on the teachings of Muhammad, who was born around 570 CE in the city of Mecca, (see page 11). Muslims believe that Allah spoke to Muhammad through an angel called Gabriel. Muhammad memorized Allah's words, which were later written down in the Qur'an, the holy book of Islam.

Muhammad was believed to be the last prophet of God. The other prophets were Adam, Noah, Abraham, Moses, and Jesus. Which other religions believe in these prophets?

The Qur'an is often put on a stand like this one.

The Five Pillars of Islam

The Five Pillars of Islam help Muslims put their faith into action. These are the five duties that Muslims must perform:

1. believe that there is no God but Allah and that Muhammad is His messenger;
2. pray five times a day—once in the morning and evening, at noon, and at two other times during the day;
3. give money to those who need help;
4. **fast**, or eat no food, from morning to evening during the month of prayer called Ramadan (Fasting reminds Muslims that others may not have food.);
5. make a pilgrimage to Mecca at least once in a lifetime (see page 11).

These men are praying at a mosque. Women pray separately. Muslims always face Mecca when they pray.

Each of these men is wearing a scarf on his head that is held in place by a black cord. Long, white shirts cover their bodies.

minaret
balcony for muezzin

*Mosques have one or more **minarets**, or tall, thin towers. A man called a **muezzin** stands high on a minaret and calls people to prayer.*

Many Muslim girls and women wear scarves on their heads and faces to show modesty.

 # What is Hinduism?

Hinduism is the oldest religion in the world! It began over 4,000 years ago in northern India. Hindus believe in one Supreme Spirit, which they call Brahman. They believe that a part of Brahman's spirit lives in every person. This part is called the *atman*, or soul. Some Hindus worship only Brahman, and some also worship hundreds of gods and goddesses. They believe that these are all parts of Brahman. The three main Hindu gods are Brahma, Vishnu, and Shiva.

(below) Brahma, who is different from Brahman, is the Creator. He has four faces and arms. (right) Vishnu is the Preserver. He is often shown with blue skin.

Shiva destroys and creates. He is also known as Lord of the Dance.

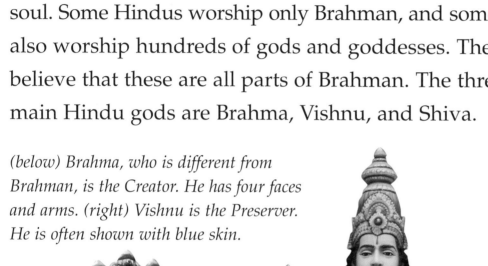

Ganesh looks like an elephant. He is the son of Shiva. People pray to Ganesh for good luck.

Some Hindus become **gurus**, or teachers. This guru is doing **yoga**. Yoga is a set of exercises that joins together the body, mind, and spirit.

This boy is taking part in a Hindu festival. He is made up to look like Vishnu. Vishnu's face is blue, like the sky. Hindus believe Vishnu is everywhere.

Most Hindus meditate each day. Some chant the sound "Om" to quiet their thoughts. The written symbol of "Om" is the symbol of Hinduism.

"Om"

Dancing is part of many Hindu festivals.

21

What is Sikhism?

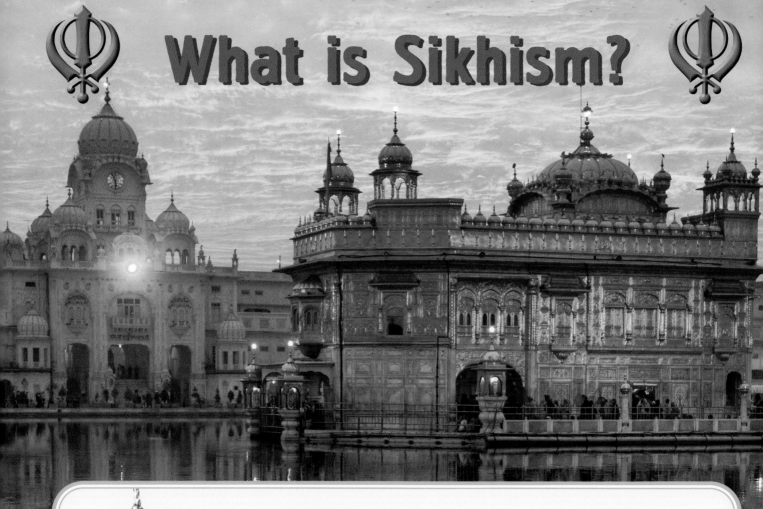

Guru Nanak's picture

A man named Guru Nanak founded the Sikh religion. There were nine other gurus after him. When the last guru, Guru Gobind Singh, died, the Sikh holy book, *Guru Granth Sahib*, became the final guru. The most sacred place for Sikhs is the Golden Temple, shown above. The Golden Temple is open on all four sides and is surrounded by water. It is in Amritsar, in northern India, near Pakistan. Most Sikhs try to visit this temple at least once in their lifetime and bathe in the holy water. They believe that the water cleanses away people's bad deeds.

Sikh worship

A Sikh temple is called a *gurdwara*. Each temple has a room for worship. People gather there to read from the holy book and to sing songs. Sikhs believe in one God. They pray and meditate each day. They do not have a special day for worship.

*Sikh men and some women wear **turbans**. Turbans are long scarves that are wrapped around the head.*

Close communities

A Sikh temple also has a kitchen and dining hall, where people cook and eat together. Sikhs believe that all people are equal. They have a very strong sense of community. They enjoy being together and look after one another.

These women are cooking a meal for many people. Sikhs often share meals in their temple dining halls.

Diwali is a festival of lights in India. Lamps are lit, and there are fireworks. Sikhs place lamps around the Golden Temple to celebrate the day that the sixth Sikh Guru was freed from prison.

What is Buddhism?

Buddhism began in India about 2,500 years ago. Buddhism is based on the teachings of Siddhartha Gautama, a man who became known as the Buddha. Buddha means "Enlightened One." Buddhists believe that the purpose in life is to find **enlightenment**. Being enlightened means having a feeling of freedom and pure joy. Buddhists do not believe in a god, and they do not worship Buddha. They respect him and follow his teachings. Buddhists care about all living things and treat them with kindness.

In this picture, the Buddha is sitting on a lotus flower. Lotus flowers grow in mud and rise into sunlight above water. Buddhists believe that people can rise into enlightenment by following the teachings of Buddha.

Buddhists believe that we suffer when we are selfish and do not think of others. The cure for suffering is the Eightfold Path.

The Eightfold Path

1. **Right view**: Understand what is real in life.
2. **Right thought**: Think about others.
3. **Right speech**: Tell the truth and say kind things.
4. **Right action**: Be kind and helpful to others.
5. **Right work**: Do jobs that help others and which do not harm living things.
6. **Right effort**: Live wisely.
7. **Right attention**: Be aware of your thoughts and how you are acting.
8. **Right concentration**: Spend time being quiet and listen to your inner guide. Make good choices.

*Buddhists who live in Tibet make beautiful **mandalas**, or designs, from colored sand. After the mandalas are finished and seen by others, they are destroyed to show that life is constantly changing and that nothing is permanent.*

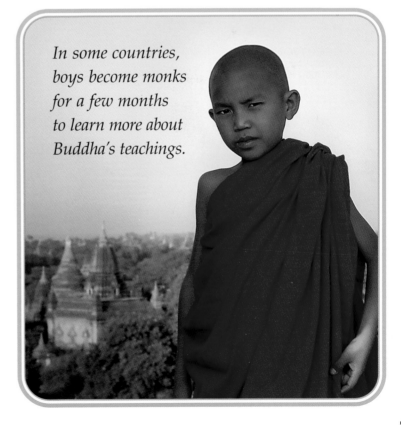

In some countries, boys become monks for a few months to learn more about Buddha's teachings.

Religions of East Asia

Confucius believed that we should treat others the way we would like to be treated—with kindness and respect.

East Asia includes countries such as China, Japan, Taiwan, Vietnam, and Korea. The people in these countries practice religions such as Buddhism, Confucianism, Taoism, and folk religions. Confucianism taught people to live quietly and peacefully and to respect their parents and **ancestors**. Taoism is a belief that life flows like a river, and people who flow with it have easy lives. The yin-yang symbol of Taoism shows two forces working together in everything. Folk religions celebrate the spirits of nature. People pray to the spirits for help.

Guanyin is part of Buddhism, Taoism, and folk religions. She is also known as the Goddess of Mercy because people believe she listens to their problems and helps them. In this picture, her statue is on a lotus flower that sits on the tails of several dragons.

Guanyin

The yin-yang symbol shows that everything has two sides that balance each other.

Shinto

Many Japanese people are Buddhists, but they also believe in Shinto. Shinto is Japan's **ancient**, or very old, religion. It is a belief that everything in nature has energy and power. The energy comes from spirits called *kami*. Shinto has many festivals that honor the *kami*. One of the favorite spring celebrations is the Cherry Blossom Festival. When the cherry trees blossom in spring, people have picnics in the parks where many cherry trees grow.

This girl is doing a traditional Japanese dance during the Cherry Blossom Festival. This holiday is now celebrated in many countries where Japanese people live.

This boy is dressed in a traditional Japanese kimono.

These children are part of a parade in the Hakata Gion Yamakasa festival, a summer celebration that takes place in Fukuoka, Japan.

Native American beliefs

Native North American people belong to many **nations**. A nation is a group of people who share a set of beliefs, traditions, and way of life. Native North Americans have different traditions, but most believe that living and non-living things are connected because they all come from the Creator or Great Spirit. Native people feel that it is important to treat plants, animals, one another, and the land with respect. Part of that respect is being thankful and not wasting Earth's gifts.

*Native people have great respect for their **elders**. Elders are the old or wise members of their communities. Teachings and traditions are passed down through the stories of the elders.*

(right) People from some Native nations along the Pacific coast of Canada and the United States carve **totem poles** made from tree trunks. The totem poles show images of the powerful animal spirits that are part of families or Native groups.

(above) Some Native children go on **vision quests**, or journeys, before they become teenagers. When a child is ready, he or she goes alone into the wilderness and fasts for a number of days. A guardian animal usually comes in a dream and shows the child the path that he or she needs to take in life. After returning home, the child is considered to be an adult. Vision quests teach children to be brave. They also give them a better understanding of who they are inside and what is important in their own lives.

(left) The Medicine Wheel shows that life is a circle that has no end. The directions at the center of the circle stand for north, south, east, and west, with Mother Earth below, and Father Sky above. The Medicine Wheel represents harmony and connection among all living things on Earth.

Respecting one another

People are the same because we are different! Religion is one of the differences that make us the same—the same because we all want to live good lives, even though we may choose different ways to do that. Sometimes, our different beliefs have led us to hurt one another. At other times, they have led us to help one another in amazing ways! Our schools and communities are made up of people from many faiths. The only way we can live happily together is to respect one another's beliefs and ways of life. Whether you have a religion or not, the best way to show your beliefs is to live them and to allow others to do the same. Below are ideas that have come from different religions. What other ideas or actions would you add to this list?

Ideas to live by

- Help those who need help.
- Spend quiet time alone every day to become aware of your thoughts and actions.
- Be kind and respectful to others. Honor your parents, teachers, and other adults.
- Flow like a river. Do not not fight everyone and everything!
- Be happy, smile, laugh, and have fun. Love yourself and others.
- Know that we are connected to everyone and everything on Earth. Help take care of Earth, our home!

Glossary

Note: Some boldfaced words are defined where they appear in the book.

ancestor A relative of someone, usually older than a grandparent

ancient Something that is very old

covenant A bargain or promise

elder An older, respected member of a tribe or village

fast To eat only certain foods or no food at all

holy Referring to the worship of God

pilgrim A person who travels to a place for worship

meditate To sit in silence and empty one's mind of thoughts

Messiah The promised savior of the Jewish people; also refers to Jesus Christ

resurrected To be raised from the dead

sacred Something that has come from or has to do with God or gods

shrine A place of worship

stable A building where farm animals live

symbol Something that stands for something else

turban A long piece of cloth that is wrapped around the head

Index

Bible 8, 9, 14, 15, 17
Brahman 20
Buddha 9, 24, 25
Buddhism/Buddhists 7, 8, 9, 24–25, 26, 27
Christianity/Christians 6, 8, 9, 10, 11, 14–15, 16–17
churches 16, 17
Confucianism 7, 26
folk religions 26
God/gods 4, 5, 6, 7, 8, 12, 13, 14, 15, 18, 19, 20, 23, 24, 26
Guru Granth Sahib 8, 22

Guru Nanak 22
gurus 21, 22, 23
Hinduism/Hindus 6, 8, 11, 20–21
holidays 9, 13, 14, 15, 17, 27
Islam/Muslims 6, 8, 10, 11, 18–19
Jesus Christ 6, 9, 10, 14, 15, 16, 17, 18
Judaism/Jews 6, 8, 9, 10, 12–13, 14
mosques 11, 19
Muhammad 18, 19

Native Americans 7, 28–29
Passover 9, 13
prayers 4, 5, 10, 13, 19, 20, 23, 26
Qur'an 8, 18
sacred places 10–11, 22, 23
Shinto 7, 27
Sikhism/Sikhs 6, 8, 22–23
synagogues 13
Taoism 7, 8, 26
temples 10, 13, 22, 23
Torah 9, 13

Further reading

These books will help you learn more about religion. For more information about the books, look for them in your library or go to **www.crabtreebooks.com**.

Refugee Child is the exciting story of author Bobbie Kalman's experiences during the Hungarian Revolution, her middle-of-the-night escape across the border to Austria, and her life as a refugee and immigrant. Bobbie overcame many obstacles on her way to becoming an author of hundreds of children's books. Parts of *Refugee Child* focus on the religious traditions and celebrations of Christmas in Hungary and Austria. Reading level: grades 4–5.

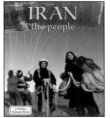

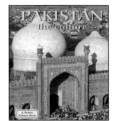

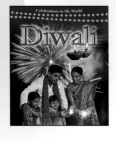

The Lands, Peoples, and Cultures series by **Bobbie Kalman**: Learn about the beliefs and ways of life of the people who live in these countries: Afghanistan, Argentina, Australia, Brazil, Canada, China, Cuba, Egypt, El Salvador, England, France, Germany, Greece, India, Iran, Iraq, Ireland, Israel, Italy, Jamaica, Japan, Mexico, Nigeria, Pakistan, Peru, Philippines, Puerto Rico, Russia, South Africa, Spain, and Vietnam. Reading level: grades 4–5.

Celebrations in My World series explores the history and traditions of major celebrations around the world, including: *Christmas, Easter, Chinese New Year, Day of the Dead, Earth Day, Halloween, Passover, Thanksgiving, Diwali, Cinco de Mayo, Ramadan, Hanukkah, Kwanzaa, Martin Luther King, Jr. Day,* and *Constitution Day.* Reading level: grades K–2.

Printed in the U.S.A.—CG